BOUND
BOOKS

Published by Bound Books in 2023.
Bound Books is an imprint of Wildling Books Ltd.
Words © Rebekah Lipp 2022. Illustrations © Craig Phillips 2022.
Edited by Nicola McCloy. 'Cosmic Threads' poem © Tracy Manu 2022.
Art direction and book design by Laura Phillips.

A catalogue record for this book is available from the National Library of New Zealand.

ISBN 978-1-99-117970-8 (paperback)
ISBN 978-1-99-117971-5 (POD)

www.wildlingbooks.com

INTUITION

It holds the answers you seek

Intuition is our ability to access knowledge from within us, without help from the outside world. Often when no one knows the 'right' thing to do, your inner compass ensures you steer your course in a certain way, or signals to you a sure 'yes' or 'no' through an internal energy.

Intuition is your superpower. It holds an immense creative energy that we can tap into to help us give meaning to our life and make a positive difference in this world. It can provide us with solutions when we know how to access the limitless knowledge that lies within us all.

This book is designed to help you connect more clearly with your source, your God, your spirituality and who you truly are. Use it to help reveal the deeper, truer you, and to connect at a soul level with all the knowledge of the universe that is held within you.

By tapping into that which you already know, you will begin to trust yourself wholly, as the magnificent being you are. Find what resonates with you, whether you find comfort in your intuition being your god's voice and guidance, or that of a collective consciousness. Your intuition just 'knows' and I believe that it is an energy that connects us all. All living creatures, plants, the Earth and the universe/God — everything is one and everything is connected.

Our intuition is our inner compass, there to gently guide us along our path

It saddens me to see so many people who have lost the ability to be guided by their intuition, or even to be able to access it at all. They are unable to use it as a compass through life's journey on Earth. No longer trusting of themselves, they are unable to hear and connect with their inner wisdom. It happens when we let other people tell us what is good for us.

Over time, that loss of trust in ourselves compounds, and we find ourselves more reliant on others to tell us how to lead our lives. If we stop for just a moment and tune into our intuition, we will know what to do without having to ask or be told by others.

As a young child, I had a strong connection with my intuition. Over the years, however, it became redundant as I didn't feel confident to use it. Instead, I listened when I was told what to do, what to like and who I was by everyone else in my life. The more I listened to other voices, the less I was able to access my intuition and the more lost I became with no idea who I was, what I wanted to do or what my meaning and purpose were.

It was only when I had my children that my inner knowing started to return. To this day, I regret making choices that went against my intuition when my children were young. Instead of trusting what I felt and knew to be right for me and my babies, I was often pressured by others to choose an alternative. As I can't go back and choose differently, now I search for the lessons to be found in the decisions I made.

It is through these decisions that we learn just how important it is to become connected with ourselves — that deep soul connection, that trusting in ourselves, that inner guidance which has our best interests at heart. No one else can know what is best for us more than ourselves, so it is time to start trusting and believing that you can make the choices that are best for you and your future.

Sometimes it can feel like our inner guidance is steering us off course. If I fully trust my guidance, it sometimes can send me towards zones of discomfort. The more risky it felt, the more I would make excuses to avoid making change. Deep down, though, something would keep steering me towards what I was trying to avoid doing.

Once I started to piece everything together, the signs became so obvious that it was clear that deep feeling within had almost been yelling at me to act. It was like I was being slapped about the face by the universe, which was trying to wake me up so I could see the path ahead. When these big shifts began to happen, I learned I just had to trust myself even when I had no idea what was ahead.

Once I'd made the decision to move forward, a period of uncertainty and sometimes even panic followed. But once I got through that zone of discomfort, the way started to become clear and what unfolded has led me to places of fulfilment and meaning that I couldn't have imagined when I'd set out.

Each time I trusted these big shifts, I grew as a person and became more connected spiritually to who I am and why I am here. Many people are searching, trying to find a path towards a place of meaning and fulfilment, asking themselves 'Why am I here?' 'What is my true purpose?' and 'What should I be doing?'

Each of us is experiencing a different journey. Millions of journeys are happening across the planet right now, just as millions of journeys have happened in the past and millions of journeys will happen in the future. All that energy and all that knowledge can be accessed. That is what I believe and what my ancestors believed. When I write these words, I feel it within me – in my belly, heart and throat. The energy within rises and lets me know it is true.

Everyone is the centre of their own universe

For a very long time, I have felt a disconnect – I didn't feel like I belonged here. The older I got, the more I felt this.

However, at a young age, I was deeply connected with my inner knowing without even realising. I believed that everyone was the centre of their own universe. My inability to articulate my ideas clearly as I was so young meant that I described feeling like I was the centre of the universe and that when I fell asleep at night, the world stopped. Things affected me, while not affecting others. As a result of this perspective, I was misunderstood and laughed at because people thought I was saying I was more special than others. Instead, I meant that we all are special, that every single person on the planet is the centre of their own universe.

I was extremely sensitive as a child and I soaked up energy from all around me. Once, when I was small, my grandmother told me she could see my beautiful aura and that I was a healer. She was Catholic and always had pictures of the pope and Mother Teresa hanging up on the walls. She was also very spiritual. She was also very psychic and had predicted some pretty remarkable events over her lifetime. She used to read tea leaves, connect with those past on and had vivid dreams with messages of the future. She opened this world up to me and helped me understand that there is so much more than meets the eye. I am sure she was a spirit guide as she was one of only a few people with whom I experienced unconditional love. With her, I could just be me and she didn't want to change me. I miss her and feel her presence often.

As an adult, I discovered I am an empath, as are many of you who are reading this, I'm sure. This book called to you and you connected with its energy. Your intuition has led you here for a reason. What could it be?

My intuition keeps leading me to ways I can help heal others, ways I could use my sensitivity and emotional awareness. I love coming up with ideas and ways to enrich other people's lives. I have always had a deep sense of wanting to help others, as is so often the way with sensitive people or empaths. For me, part of the process towards really becoming 'tuned in' was removing the labels that others had placed on me. These labels were limiting me and preventing me from trusting my soul guidance. They prevented me from really knowing myself and, in turn, trusting myself. They blocked me from accessing the messages my intuition was giving me. When I look back, God was, and still is, giving me subtle clues. If I am awake enough to notice them, they show me a path that I can follow.

Even though I still feel like I don't belong here, the more work I do to strengthen my connection with my inner knowing, the more content I feel. I now have a sense of meaning and belonging which I have lacked for so long. I feel part of something much greater. I am so thankful to have committed to myself to do the work needed to rekindle this connection again. The connection I was born with.

Intuition doesn't speak to us, it moves us

The older I've got, the more in tune with my inner wisdom I have become. When I don't listen to it, I regret it and often end up kicking myself for going against my inner guide. I should know better by now!

At times, I have let the world, stress and my ego take over. When that happens I second guess myself, losing trust in myself. During these times, I get confused between my anxiety and my intuition. What if I'm wrong? What if I try to trust my inner knowing and instead it is my fear talking to me? Am I just really stressed right now?

Instinct or intuition?

Instincts are primal and tend to kick in when survival is at stake. In emergency situations, your instincts take over to keep you alive. Instincts are a natural response, an inborn tendency that is there to protect you. This inborn behaviour can be activated by numerous different triggers.

Your intuition does not react like instincts do. Instead, it is more of a messenger. While instinct pushes you to take action, intuition gives you a gentle nudge towards a line of thought, which may then lead to you taking action. Your intuition taps into the experiences of your life and, some believe, the experiences of all lives.

How to tap into your intuition

Your intuition needs to be used regularly. The more you use it, the stronger it becomes. You can use it to do simple tasks at first and then, as you trust yourself more, you can tap into a much deeper knowledge – a knowledge that you could never have imagined has always been held within you. You are a powerful vessel of knowledge and wisdom. We all are.

It's time to start noticing, to start listening to that which has no words but moves us by using energy. My intuition never speaks as words tend to come from my ego, and that mind chatter is often not factual or helpful. My intuition, however, takes the shape of a physical feeling that spreads through my core. It's an energy that pulls or pushes me. The more you practise tuning into your body and becoming more connected, the more you can strengthen that body–soul connection.

When you first start actively using your intuition, start with small choices that won't matter if you get them wrong – things like 'Shall I go for a walk?' or 'Should I spend time with a certain person?' Observe what registers within you and how you feel.

Once you start connecting and making small choices, you will become more aware of what feels right deep inside. This will help you to build up a sense of trust in yourself. The more you use your intuition, the easier it becomes for you to dial into it through feelings, images, smells, sounds, synchronicities, signs and symbols.

Your intuition is your link to the collective consciousness, to your spirituality, your God or gods, to the light and love shining within you, to the all-knowing wisdom.

To understand your purpose or find more meaning, listen to the whispers from your soul and look for the clues that the universe scatters before you

The world seems to have become increasingly divided. It feels angrier. But at the same time there is a bright energy of hope, of change, of elevation. I have been using this time to connect deeper with the spiritual side of me. Drawing from my Celtic and Viking ancestors and the knowing they used to survive, I have committed to fully trusting myself. I have made a conscious effort to tap into my intuition every chance I get. This has led me to make choices that are completely against the collective, but I am trusting that I just know what is right for me and, in time, I know I will be rewarded or will understand the reason why I felt compelled to do what I have done.

I feel like this time of change that is upon us is here to help awaken those who have lost connection, to help us move towards living in a way that unites us. By this I mean, we should once again create connection within our local communities and with the land on which we live. We should elevate and honour each other, even if we have different beliefs. We need to focus on the common connection of being human and on allowing each person to have their own individual human experience in whichever way they need.

At times while writing this book, it has seemed as though the words have come from out of nowhere, like they were waiting to be written. When this has happened, I have trusted that this is what needs to be included. It was as if this book had been gifted to me from the universe – a gift for me to share in order to help others connect to their spiritual side.

Your intuition may give you premonitions of the future, glimpses of what might be ahead

This book is a way for me to send my love and gratitude to all of my ancestors, who had strong connections to their God/s, to the animals and plants, and to the Earth. I reach out to them, knowing they are close by. I feel their love and support.

We can create new ties to those ancestors who have been cut from us. We can create new traditions and rituals that connect us once again to our deep spirituality, which we may have lost. We can use our inner energy, which is connected to the past, to guide us back to the knowledge that our ancestors held strong. With this connection I send back love to my ancestors and those passed on. I am creating, in my own way, ways to reach out to them.

So much has been lost – traditions, language, rituals. However, I believe that how we connect isn't as important as the intention behind what we do. Don't ever feel you are practising your spirituality wrong. Do what feels right for you. Trust yourself.

Everything is connected. Everything is of value. You can find a deeper meaning everywhere. Start looking and be open to the signs around you. Use this book to help guide you, to heal you, to help you find your place in this world. Use it to find the answers you seek.

Ultimately, I want my intuition to guide me to my truth. I hope this book can help you to find your truth too, through the wisdom of your intuition.

Bex

WAYS TO USE THIS BOOK

Initially, I thought about just creating an oracle deck of cards, but my intuition called for me to expand that deck into a book – this book!

You can use this book as you would an oracle deck, by flicking to any page and gaining some instant wisdom that might be calling out to you from within. You can pair the book with the Intuition Card Deck, so the card set can give you more guidance, or you can use the book to expand upon what the card deck might be telling you.

This book provides a beautiful reminder for you to practise using your intuition. It is full of ideas for you to explore further. If something resonates with you, try to examine why. It is here to assist you to find the answers that you seek, a reminder to go deeper within yourself. It is a tool to help you uncover more about who you are and what you are here for.

You can use the book to ask yourself a question or to ask for something more specific. Ask for a sign then flick to a page. Your intuition will let you know if the page you land on says what you need to hear. If it doesn't feel right, flick to another page.

Throughout the book, I have included different exercises for you to try. Only try them if you feel a connection. Again, you will know in that moment if they are right for you to do. The exercises are there to help you to work more deeply on your connection with your inner knowing. You may find the answers you seek after completing an exercise or two. Each entry also has a space for signs. These words give you a quick reference for what's on the page you have turned to. Having read the entry, you can then take time to focus on the list of signs to see if any synchronicities align with them.

WAYS TO CHECK IN WITH YOUR INTUITION

Body check

How does your body feel? What is it trying to communicate with you? When you have spent time with someone, how do you feel afterwards? Are you drained or do you feel energised? Your higher self is giving you insights via your body and your emotions. Check in with yourself after certain activities and see what messages your intuition is trying to give you.

Remember that your intuition should feel light and unemotional. When you listen to your intuition, it should leave you feeling calm and with a clear sensation in your body – this is often a sensation of a 'yes' or a 'no'.

Exercise:
Do a body scan at least once a week. Are you tense in any areas of your body? Regularly checking in with your body will help you to connect more with your intuition. As so many messages come through our physical body, learning to be aware of changes within it may help you link those messages with what is happening in your life.

Stand with your feet shoulder-width apart. With bare feet, start tapping your heels into the earth by lifting them up and down, while the front of your feet remain on the ground. Bring that stale energy up, shaking it up your legs and body. Shake out the energy from your arms and hands. Shake it up and out, just like a cat or dog shakes their body. Once you have released the old, trapped energy, take some deep breaths, breathing in fresh energy.

Laugh

Laughter really connects you with your intuition. When you laugh, you become more open and more conscious, and it will lift your frequency. Laughter's beautiful, positive energy creates a strong connection with your inner knowing. It enables you to walk lighter and be open to suggestions from the universe or your God or gods. When was the last time you really laughed? How can you invite more laughter into your life?

Yes/no sway

A few different people have shown me the yes/no sway as a method to help me ask for answers and tap into my inner knowing. The more I use this as an intuition guide, the more astounded I have been with how my body knows the answers before my mind does. There is energy that pushes and pulls – it knows, it is connected.

Exercise:
Stand with your feet shoulder-width apart and relax. Ask yourself a simple question that you know the answer to. Feel your body move either slightly forward, which means 'yes', or slightly back, which means 'no'.

Some believe that the body is deeply linked to the subconscious mind. That the body has memories held within your muscles and this is how the exercise can work. It is as though your body holds the answers through that direct link to the subconscious.

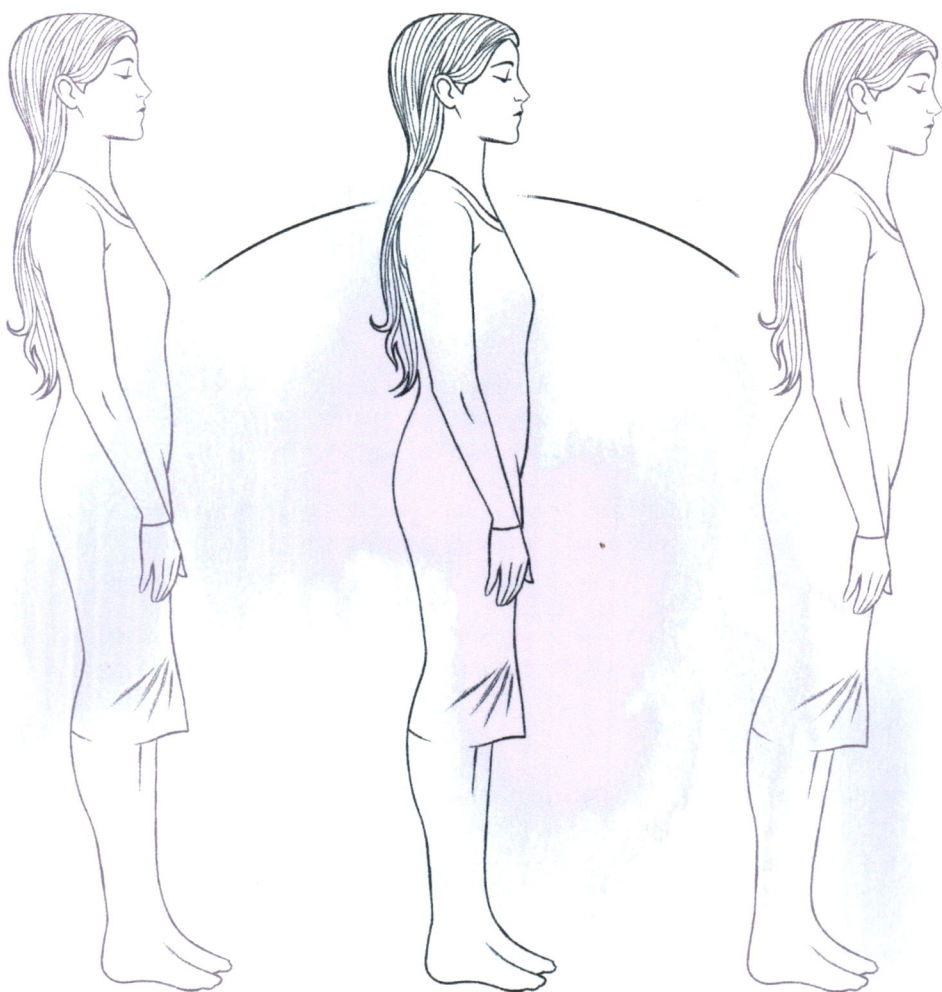

Intuition time

Have some quiet time away from the noise of the world. Set aside time each day to tune into your intuition. Ask it some questions and notice how you feel. Sit with yourself. Use this time to complete some of the practices in this book. What thoughts come up after doing some of the exercises? Ask your intuition for guidance. Ask for a sign to appear for you during the day.

Keep an intuition notebook

Do you sense a particular message coming through or do you have a gut feeling about something? Write it all down. It doesn't need to make sense. It could be just words or questions or feelings you are experiencing – whatever it is, throw it all down on paper.

Use an intuition notebook to explore why things have come up for you. It can be a place where you can make notes, record signs that you notice and write about dreams that you have. By writing things down, you're giving yourself a chance to delve deeper into the meaning of these things.

After a period of time, you may be able to look at these notes and see them come together into a coherent message.

Keep a dream notebook

Beside your bed, keep a notebook and pen so that when you wake, you can write down anything you remember about the dreams you've had. This will help you to work out what your subconscious mind is pondering while you sleep. Sometimes you may just remember small things, other times you may remember more lengthy scenes. Jot down whatever you recall and, over time, these notes may start making more sense to you.

Signs

When signs or synchronicities appear during the day, take note of what you were thinking at the time. What were you doing when you noticed the sign? Start piecing this information together. What are the signs trying to tell you?

These signs come in ways that seem a little 'off' but in a good way. They might be in the form of repeating numbers, like when you keep checking the time and it is 11:11, 2:22 or 5:55. They could come in the form of feathers or anything else that is a little unusual. They could be lyrics in a song that seem to be speaking directly to you in that moment. They could come in the form of a book with a message that resonates with you. Wherever the signs come from, they will shake your core a little at first. It may feel a little weird, but you will learn to embrace and love them.

When you notice a sign, in that moment, the universe or your God is reaching out to you. Remember to thank them for letting you know they are there for you. Send love and gratitude back for the signs you are given. This will raise your energy vibration and enable you to receive even more into your life.

We have created a beautiful intuition notebook which is available to order via our website **www.wildlingbooks.com**.

Acceptance

Acceptance is being able to accept what is, right now, and to let go of thoughts and emotional ties from the past and worries about the future. Things are as they are. There is nothing you can do in this moment other than accept what is. Acceptance helps us be in the present, which is a fantastic way to connect with our intuition. Take a moment each day to allow acceptance in. Let your worries melt away in that moment. Let your dramas dissolve. Drop all the wanting you have and just be. Fully step into the moment you are in without wanting to change anything.

Meditate

For me, practising meditation regularly is key to helping clear the clutter in my mind. I practise Transcendental Meditation and have done so for about two decades. I have found it amazing at helping me to clear my mind, relax my body and release stress. I also highly recommend the morning and evening meditations by Dr Joe Dispenza.

Meditation is a great way to bring you in closer contact with your subconscious mind. It helps to raise your vibration into a space of love, joy and inner peace. Allowing calmness into your body can enable you to hear your intuition more clearly.

Kything prayer

An almost lost Celtic practice called kything involves using prayer or thought to become connected with others or objects. It is a way to present your authentic self to another and to join together without losing your sense of self fully. Through this prayer state, you can transcend separateness and enter into a deep state of unconditional love and connectedness.

Exercise:
Using your imagination focus your thoughts on an object or person. Next, bring yourself into your field of thoughts. Surround yourself with glorious, loving energy from the universe. Imagine golden light filling your body until you are glowing. Now bring into focus the object or person you want to connect with. Now both of you are sharing the same space. Using your imagination, allow the golden light that is filling your body with unconditional love to start wrapping around and filling the object or person. Hold both yourself and the object or person in your mind together wrapped in swirling love light energy. Feel the connection, the togetherness, the oneness. Say a blessing or give thanks to be sharing space together. Hold onto this moment for as long as you want.

HOW TO RAISE YOUR VIBRATION

What does it mean to raise your vibration? How can we do this? I like to think about our thoughts and emotions as energy, like everything in the universe. Different emotions have different vibrations. For example, the emotions of anger or resentment have lower vibrations compared to those of joy and love.

If you wish to raise your vibration, the best and easiest way to do this is to change your thoughts and, in turn, your emotions will change too.

By spending some time each day visualising a future that is filled with love, acceptance and joy, you will naturally raise your vibration, even if it's just for a small amount of time. These emotions and thoughts then attract more of that which you transmit into the world. So, start sending out the signals of love and joy!

Be aware of what food and toxins you allow into your body. Eliminating things like alcohol, chemicals and processed foods will help to raise your vibrations. Treat your body like the temple it is for it houses your divine spirit.

Dance and sing, do the things that welcome joy into your life and your energy will vibrate at a higher frequency, making you feel lighter, more connected and at ease with yourself and the world around you.

Learning to trust your intuition can be transformational

I have learned that trusting my intuition can open me up to new opportunities and pathways in my life. It has led me to make difficult choices with unknown results, that have caused me to tread an uncertain path for a while before taking me to a more enlightened and fulfilling life – a life with more meaning and purpose than I could ever have dreamed.

My intuition is like having a mentor within me, always there to help me make wiser choices and in turn helping me trust myself more and creating more confidence as I continue my journey. It helps me be more intentional about what I do. As a result, I have more of an awareness about what really matters and, at the same time, a deeper understanding of who I am and what I am here for.

Being connected with my intuition has allowed me to find the extraordinary in the mundane, to marvel at the beauty I am surrounded with, to have a deep sense of gratitude in the most basic of experiences, even the uncomfortable ones. It truly heightens all levels of the human journey.

Live your life in a state of wonder and awe at the true blessing it is to be alive in this moment.

INTUITION

CONTENTS

SURRENDER

Time to release what is no longer serving you

Relax into your body and soul. Learning to truly surrender allows you to fully accept what is happening – no judgement, no sides taken. Simply being able to express what is happening right in this moment.

With this acceptance, you can stop yourself from struggling against what is. Stop battling to change and instead simply surrender to this moment. Change will come one way or another, but to surrender is to let go of the fight. Doing this may allow you time to see the other options, to try something different to get a different outcome, to acknowledge that resistance could be a frequency of energy that isn't helpful to you.

Surrender doesn't mean giving up, but simply giving in to this moment in order to change the energy within you.

Allow the control that you wish to hold onto to be released. You cannot always control outcomes in life. Everything is as it should be – even in difficult moments. It can be those moments that lead to the change within that brings us the life we desire or allows us to discover who we truly are. Great strength can be found when we surrender.

Stop thinking and surrender to the wisdom that lies within. There you will find peace, connection and answers.

Exercise:
Take a deep breath in through your nose and slowly breathe out your mouth as if you were blowing out of a straw. Repeat five times. Say, 'I surrender to this moment. I accept where I am on my journey. I let go of the struggle to control. I know the universe is working for me and I will stop struggling against it. I surrender to this moment and feel my soul lighten. Every time I breathe out, I let go and feel more relaxed and freer.'

Signs: Acceptance, peace, contentment, answers

DIVINE UNITY

You are so loved and supported

You are made of the stars. You are a child of the universe, a child of God. This means you are always deeply loved and supported. If you feel as though you don't belong, are an outsider, or are different, it is time to connect with the divine in you, that which is connected to everyone and everything.

The divine is in everything and within you. You are loved from within. Close your eyes and imagine love as a bright, warm light filling up every part of your body. There is gold light swirling through you. This is a healing energy. This is the unconditional love of the universe, of your God or gods, of the source. There is no love like it on earth. It is true, pure love that is available to you any time you need it. Love from within. You are always held and supported. You are never alone.

Find magic in the mundane, and you will find magic everywhere. Bring the ordinary into the extraordinary. Marvel at the wonders of everyday life, including yourself. Every aspect of you is a miracle and should be celebrated just as God celebrates you, just as your spirit guides celebrate you.

Just as the great Rumi said, "You are not a drop in the ocean, you are the entire ocean in a drop."

As you begin to accept your part in the universe, you will notice your energy begins to become lighter. Animals are drawn to your energy as they know they are safe as it is the energy of love. Embrace this unity. Celebrate this unity. Acknowledge that you are a remarkable piece of the universe.

Exercise:
Look at yourself as a whole. Are you looking after yourself physically, mentally, and spiritually? Are there any areas where you need to help bring more balance into your general well-being?

Don't make yourself feel bad if there are areas you need to work on. Simply acknowledge that you need to care for yourself in a better way. Start putting yourself first, knowing that you deserve to be loved and cared for. What can you do today to care for yourself?

Signs: Love, unity, oneness, compassion

INNOCENCE

Time to play — let your wild child out

Stop being so serious for a while. Let the little child within you play. Have fun! Be silly! Take some time to reflect on all you have in this moment then celebrate it with joy.

Play is necessary to lift your soul. Find humour in the situation to lighten the load. Let it lift you to a higher frequency. Call on your inner child to come to the front — the one who used to play in puddles without worrying about getting wet and dirty; the one who would find magic in the smallest of places; the one who would find joy in the simplest of things; the one who lets their imagination run wild and free.

We can become stuck in our ways, so it is good to do things that push us out of our comfort zones or challenge the status quo. Let your routines fall away for a moment. Be spontaneous and see what adventures are to be had and memories are to be made by your playful soul.

When you return to innocence you can let the universe surprise you. God's messages could be right there waiting to be discovered through play. No expectations — just let your soul be carefree and wild.

Become more open to the wonder that surrounds you in everyday things. Play can strengthen your connection with your intuition, which in turn sparks creativity. You may look at things with a new perspective. Possibilities might open up before your eyes.

Exercise:
Try something completely new. Learn a musical instrument. Play a board game. Play a game with your children. Go bowling or get on a trampoline. Run through a sprinkler on a summer's day. Walk in the rain and jump in puddles.

Signs: Carefree, playful, spontaneous, joy, humour, fun, creativity

SEER

A message is on its way

Someone is trying to pass on an important message. Be sure to listen. It could come from the most unexpected places. It could be a dream, a vision, or even the lyrics of a song that speak to you. It might come in the form of a random sign on the street or an animal that suddenly appears. Pay attention to your dreams and to things that seem out of place during the day.

If you tune into your intuition, you will know that this is a message for you. Don't doubt it and don't doubt yourself. You hold wisdom and knowledge deep within you. The more you connect with this wisdom, the more you will be able to see and the more messages you will hear.

Be open to receiving messages from others too. It may be a card reading from someone you know or simply someone new who has just popped up in your life.

Be open to opportunities that invite different people into your life. A seer is near and their abilities can provide information to you from the spirits. They are able to see glimpses of your potential future and can help guide you to your true path.

Listen for the wisdom the universe is trying to give to you. This wisdom can come to you in the most unexpected of ways.

Exercise:
The power you hold within can be witnessed if you believe. You can test this by picking something like a feather, a specific type of bird, or anything that means something to you. Then ask the universe or your God/gods to show you that you do in fact hold a connection within you. If, for example, you pick an animal, it may come to you on a tv show, or through a photo. The form will not always be as you might expect it., so be open to the message. If you're wondering if the message is true, try the yes/no sway intuition guide that is described on page 12. Your intuition will give you the answer.

Signs: Messages, signs, connection, guidance

WITNESS

Quietly watch those around you

Be a witness to your own life. Witness the actions of those around you, as this shows you who they really are. Be aware of how others speak. Do they speak ill of others? Are their words full of judgement and hate or are they full of optimism and gratitude? Consider that there is a chance they could speak the same way about you. When you watch how others act and what they say, it can tell you a lot about them as a person.

Using that information, start thinking about the vibrational energy of those around you. What are you allowing into your space? Does their energy vibrate at a level that elevates you or brings your energy down? The Earth needs all people to elevate to a higher level of frequency, to frequencies of love, joy and compassion. We all play a part. We must let go of frequencies of fear, greed and anger. It is therefore massively important to consider who you spend your time with. When times are tough, who is there for you?

Stand back and be a witness to yourself and the words you speak of others. How do you treat others? What frequency are you transmitting into the world? Are you celebrating others and showing your love and gratitude?

It is okay to protect your energy and simply wait for others to meet you where you are. It doesn't help anyone or the world to allow others to bring your energy down. It isn't your responsibility to lift others up. Instead, it is their responsibility to do the work to elevate themselves. You can simply be a role model and continue to work on your vibration. What can you do to lift your vibration? Be aware of who you spend time with. You must continue to be a witness.

Exercise:
Write a list of things you are grateful for, then write a list of people who elevate your energy. Take a moment to really focus on these things and these people and feel gratitude. Place your hand on your heart. Send them loving energy and allow your body to energise with love and gratitude.

Signs: *Witness, observe, frequency, vibrations*

FREEDOM

Boundless energy, light and love

We are being guided and protected. Our soul yearns for freedom to walk lightly on this Earth – so lightly that we almost lift off. That sense of freedom, of boundless energy which wants to burst from within, wants us to soar.

This freedom comes from a place of unattachment to things, to places, to others. This freedom understands that everything is one. Everything is energy.

This freedom allows us to unburden ourselves from worries that weigh us down.

This freedom liberates the soul.

Free yourself from your mind. Release yourself from the thoughts that keep you captive.

We all have different ideas, beliefs and mindsets. We can exhaust ourselves trying to convince others to think the same or be the same as us. This will only limit us. Just be!

What others think of you is of no concern. If you are travelling your path with love, then you must accept others and their differences. They are on a different path. Let go of judgements and find acceptance of what is.

Be free to speak your truth and live as you are guided. No one owns you. Let the words of others fall away. Let the expectations of others fall away. Let the attachments fall away. There is always hope. There is always a way. Start walking lighter. Look for love every chance you get, for there you will find freedom.

When the sun rises and its light falls on your cheeks, forget everything in that moment. Feel the freedom that your soul seeks. Live lighter!

Exercise:
Put some music on and dance. Move your body. Feel the freedom within you. Allow your body to move any way it wants. Allow the music to fill your body. Tell yourself that you are loved. Imagine you are lifting off the ground as you dance.

Signs: Love, protection, guidance, liberation, release

WATER

Dip in and cleanse

Water is essential for the body, mind and spirit. The water element helps us to get in touch with our emotions, allowing them to move within us and flow to the surface. It gently washes away our current worries and stress, but also allows old emotions to flow out, leaving us feeling deeply cleansed and purified.

Water teaches us to go with the flow, to be in constant gentle movement. Go easy and flow. As we are made so much of water, we can feel almost one with the water. A belonging and peace comes from connecting with it. Allow yourself to flow in whichever direction the universe is flowing. Relax into it.

Water offers us clarity and calm, a way to discover mysteries that lie within us in a gentle and nurturing way. We started life in the womb, surrounded by a warm and comforting cocoon of loving water. We can go back to the water as much as we need during our life to find that comfort and calm again if needed.

Water is sacred. It provides healing and can be used to help release stored emotions that, over time, can impact us mentally and physically.

Exercise:
Get yourself into water. It could be a cold bath, a hot shower, a mineral pool, a lake, or the ocean. Feel the strength of water that flows around and within you. Close your eyes and feel cleansed and rejuvenated. Imagine the old, deep, stuck emotions beginning to move inside. Allow them to flow out as you move through the water. Gently move your arms and legs, imagining the emotions flowing out of your fingers and toes. Let the tears flow if needed. Release!

Signs: Comfort, emotions, cleansing, release, clarity, healing, flow

LIGHTHOUSE

You can light the way for others

It is your time to shine. If you shine bright, others will see and be drawn to you. They will witness all that you are, and you will inspire them to be bold and bright too.

We pass the light to each other. Others may have lit the way for you, now they are passing you the light. Time to step into the light and hold it high so others can see their potential, just as you have seen yours.

Give yourself time to celebrate all you have achieved and how far you have come. Attaining the light means you are finally getting to know who you are, not only accepting but loving every bit of yourself. This enables you to step into a space of embracing yourself for all your quirks and weirdness.

Free yourself of all the world expects of you and shine out who you really are with no apologies. Coming from a place of love and acceptance, know you no longer have to fit in. Shine your light on all the so-called imperfections, knowing they are actually the parts of you that matter the most, that make you who you are. No longer shying from the light, you shine brilliant, beautiful and unashamedly bright.

The world needs your light. Know that, in time, you will pass the light on to another, but never ever forget how amazing you are.

Exercise:
Say out loud, 'This is who I am. I am brilliant, beautiful and bright. I stand in the light and shine my light on the world.'

Signs: Confidence, inspiration, celebration, uniqueness

DEEPLY ROOTED

There is always more than meets the eye

There is strength that is deeply rooted within you. This strength is gained from connections that are all around us. Feel strong and grounded.

So often in life it takes a team of people. All working together to help support you on your path. Never forget them. Acknowledge that you were helped along the way.

There is so much more in our life's journey than what we see with our eyes. As we stand alone in the world, there are so many connections that we cannot see that spread out from us, just like a tree's root system spreads underground. Even though we each walk our own path, we need connection with others. Our connections that are deeply rooted can help us draw strength from others when we need it the most. When life throws curveballs and creates painful times, when we are too consumed with pain or exhaustion, our connections can help us find strength and support. They care for us and love us.

We are also deeply rooted in the Earth. We can draw so much energy by creating a greater connection with the Earth. This energy is strong and always there for us, even when other people may not be. This energy can also be accessed through our connections with animals. It is in the calm we gain from petting a cat or the love a dog gives unconditionally. Seek out this energy and it will support you on your life journey. Acknowledge there are things you cannot see but that help and guide you.

Be aware that you are also sending out connections, support and strength to others. In your life, a tiny action can affect others in ways you may not be aware of. The energy you send out into the universe by way of your thoughts also affects others. We are never alone. We are all part of something much greater. We all benefit when our thoughts and actions come from a place of love and compassion. Trying to achieve a life where love and compassion are at your centre will flow out into the world and create a ripple of support for others.

Exercise:
Remove your footwear and have your feet connected with the Earth in some way. Walk on the grass or on the beach. Go barefoot in your garden. This is called earthing or grounding, and it is known to have amazing benefits for health and well-being.

Signs: Connections, energy, earth, animals, supported

MIRROR

Take some time for reflection

What do you see from others that could be a mirror on your own life? Do you notice yourself blaming or judging other people's behaviour without thinking, 'Do I also display this behaviour?' Being able to observe and consider this is a great step for personal growth. You may not find that you display similar behaviour, but instead that you need to consider and change your reaction to it.

What are you constantly seeing in life? Why do you think that this is being shown to you over and over? Have you tried doing something differently? Your reaction is especially important as it can show how you perceive others and your awareness of yourself. Closely observe your thoughts and what you say as they reflect what is inside you.

Take time to really look at yourself. Reflection is about putting your ego aside and taking the opportunity to grow, to change your behaviours and how you react to others. Challenge yourself to take a different view than before.

There is always work to do, opportunities to grow and become a better and a more whole version of ourselves. A version that isn't quick to criticise other people's journeys but that will use what we see in others as lessons and guidance to help us to level up.

Exercise:
The next time you find yourself judging someone else, flip your perspective. Try to look at things from a different angle. Consider whether you behave in a similar way at all. Become more aware of how you react then try something different.

Signs: Reflection, self-development, perception, observe

BETRAYAL

Do your thoughts betray you?

Are your thoughts driven from a place of fear and ego? Are you betraying yourself by not being connected to your innate wisdom? Are others betraying you? It's time! Time to really be honest with others and yourself. Do you want to stay in your comfort zone, or do you want to move forward and embrace new experiences?

We cannot be fully connected to our intuition if we are not open and honest. What is it you really want? Will you do what it takes to get it, or will it remain a dream because you don't want to push yourself into a zone of discomfort?

What are you open for? Do you want to know the answers? Are you ready to share your truths with the world? Now is the time. No more lies to others or yourself. We sometimes lie to ourselves as a form of self-protection, but it needs to stop. You can handle the truth. You can do the work needed. Be open to the fact that you may have made mistakes. There are always lessons in them. Try to open up your mind to new ideas and perspectives.

Offer yourself compassion. This journey can be so difficult, which is why it is important to connect deeply, to be clear with what you want and to be honest. Don't keep anything hidden anymore. Love yourself as you are. Love the journey you have taken so far. Love yourself for all the mistakes and failures, just as you do for your successes and achievements. All of this makes you who you need to be. Love who you are in this moment.

Be careful who you open yourself up to. Look to those who are close to you. Are you loved unconditionally? If those you surround yourself with treat others with betrayal and treachery, they may subject you to the same. Tread carefully, as you do not deserve to be treated this way. Look for those who support both you and others with love.

Exercise:
Observe your thoughts and your words. If you find yourself speaking ill of yourself or others, make a point of switching that into kindness. What could you say instead? Speak kind words.

Signs: Honesty, compassion, journey, betrayal, manipulation, trickery

COMMITMENT

It's time to commit fully

It is time to make a decision — it could be about a union, a friendship, a deal or a promise to yourself. Stop making excuses and make a choice one way or another. The limbo you find yourself in is only stalling your progress.

Stop sabotaging yourself. Every time you start to make progress, do you destroy all the good energy you have invested? Do you look for faults in relationships? Do you seek out flaws in order to not commit? Are you avoiding things that need to be addressed? Why do you do that? More than anything, you are worth the commitment! You won't understand if something is worth it or not until you commit fully. A half effort isn't going to prove anything at all. Give it everything or don't give anything at all.

Commit fully to what you feel drawn to. Leap in with enthusiasm and eagerness to learn and grow. We cannot always know what is 'right' or 'wrong', but a decision needs to be made nonetheless.

A commitment made now will be powerful in your journey ahead, but any commitment made requires you to play your part. Are you ready for this? Ask yourself, 'Why am I committing to this? Is this to please others or am I doing this led by my spirit or higher self?'

Exercise:
A fun way to see if your decision is what your heart desires is to play heads or tails. Assign your choices to heads and tails, then flip the coin to see where it lands.

When you receive the answer, what is your first feeling? Is it joy or disappointment? Fear or excitement? This is your body giving you a sign as to what it is you genuinely want to do.

Signs: Commitment, decisions, union, promises, fulfilment, partnership, harmony

DEEP KNOWLEDGE

There is great wisdom and creativity in you

Our thoughts can poison us, especially when we allow them space and leave them unchecked. However, thoughts aren't facts. There is knowledge much deeper that doesn't cause us stress and anxiety. That doesn't prevent us from trying new things or getting creative. Draw on the knowledge you hold within from all those who stood before you. It dwells deep down and has our best interest at heart. It doesn't speak, it moves. It won't clutter your mind.

When we are able to channel this wisdom, we do so from a place of peace and connection, and we are not driven by emotions at all. This state helps provide a clarity of thought and a great connection with the creativity that runs through our veins. We are all creative beings. We are constantly creating the reality we are experiencing.

When you start to connect to that wisdom you will understand that to live life fully is to express ourselves creatively, pursue inner peace by letting go of the judgements of others and expand the light we discover within onto others. You will also learn to let go of expectations around how things should be as these only draw you further away from the wisdom you hold. There is no set way to create or live your life.

To be wise is to be guided by imagination, love, compassion and empathy, and a sense of knowing that you are supported. You are not alone on this journey. There is help within. Trust this and trust yourself.

Have faith that what belongs to you will find you. Things will work out just as they are meant to, unfolding in perfect ways that may not make sense now. Your inner wisdom wants you to believe that everything will become clear in time. Trust in the creative ideas that stem from the deep knowledge within. What is within you now that is bursting to be created? Draw on that deep wisdom.

Exercise:
Get creative! Allow yourself to be guided organically. Don't push yourself to do things that don't flow. Grab some paint brushes or a pencil and start sketching. If you prefer, try modelling with clay. Start writing the book you've dreamed of. Allow space to be creative. The more you give yourself time to do this, the easier it will become.

Signs: Faith, support, peace, expression, trust, creativity

OBSTACLE

Challenges lie ahead

We all experience challenging times in our lives. Challenges can come at us in minor or major ways. If you notice the same challenges appearing repeatedly, dwell on what lesson that obstacle might contain.

Every problem we face is an opportunity. These challenges can be gifts that help us to improve our life. These challenges are a chance to become a better person and to grow.

Challenging times can lower your motivation and energy levels, making every move you make harder. Remember the strength that lies within you. Know that every obstacle contains lessons to be learned. These lessons might be exactly what you need to continue your soul's work. How could you use these obstacles in a meaningful way in order to help others? These obstacles can bring qualities and traits to the surface that you might not have believed existed within you. You need to progress forward to see them.

Are you creating your own obstacles? Maybe this is a sign to drop your need to be perfect or to have everything mapped out. Are you sabotaging yourself because you don't feel worthy? Are your emotions creating challenges for you? Don't let fear hold you back. Don't let unhelpful thoughts hold you back. Don't give up!

Do you dive headfirst into any obstacles that come your way, or do you run from them? Notice your behaviour during challenging times. Give yourself time to work through your choices. Know that you are always supported and loved through the energy of the universe, through your God or gods. Nothing is given to you that you cannot overcome. After we've traversed difficulties, we often recognise how much soul growth we've had. Look back on how far you have come already.

Exercise:
Write about whatever obstacle you are facing. Ask yourself if there is anything you can do to overcome it right away. Do you need help? Make a plan for how you might tackle it. Thank the universe for the lesson currently before you.

Signs: *Choices, challenges, change, meaning, life's path*

GODDESS

You are connected to the divine

The goddess understands that there are phases in life. Each phase provides important lessons that can be carried forward. However, with each phase we almost become a new person. Allowing ourselves to transition and change is part of self-growth. We can mature and see things from new perspectives as we learn more lessons in life.

What phase are you in currently? What lessons need to be learned here to help you progress to the next stage? Are you ready to move into a new phase?

Be gentle as you transition from one phase into another. It can be hard to walk away from one version of yourself in order to embrace a new cycle. However, nature teaches us all about cycles – the cycle of life and death, the cycles of the moon and sun. Energy is constantly moving and this must be embraced as a beautiful and sacred part of life.

Nature doesn't resist the cycles but understands that they are the natural process of all things. Are you resisting the natural order of things? Should you be welcoming the changes that lie ahead?

The goddess is calm, confident and willing to evolve. She knows that everything is connected. She has all she needs within her. She is gentle and compassionate. She holds a oneness in her heart.

This is a sign of inner strength and support from the divine. You are miraculous and are becoming more in tune with your spirituality. No longer deny it or fight it. You hold so much power and wisdom within. Walk tall, knowing you walk with the divine within you.

Exercise:
Say out loud, 'I honour and respect myself, knowing I hold the goddess within me. I will no longer resist change but embrace it. I understand that change is necessary for me to evolve.' Take time to think about the phase or cycle you are currently in. Could you be transitioning from that phase into a new one?

Signs: Phases, resistance, new perspectives, evolving

SUN

Radiate joy from being in alignment

The masculine and feminine are in balance within you. You are becoming fully aligned and, with this, you will find joy and contentment. You radiate happiness, and this energy attracts abundance and success to you.

There is a harmony coming into your life. Love, light and warmth is wrapped around you. There is a sense of celebration ahead. All your work is paying off and you are feeling a sense of renewed motivation to keep moving forward.

Give gratitude for all you have in this moment. This contentment and joy are to be cherished. Spread your happiness to those around you. Help others find the joy you feel through your balanced energy.

Invite optimism into your life. What will the universe offer up for you to celebrate? Have faith that success and good fortune are just around the corner. When you come into alignment, everything will flow. You will be able to manifest more easily. You will see signs everywhere indicating that you are in alignment. Use this alignment to bring in abundance.

Ask God for what you want from this life. Feel the joy of receiving within your soul, even before you have got it. Act like you are winning with every step you take. Be excited. Dream about your ultimate future and trust that it will come true.

Everything is lining up. Everything is falling into place. The time of uncertainty is over as a clear way forward is forged through the energy of your alignment. Go for it! Seize the day with vitality and a grateful heart.

Exercise:
Get out into the sunshine. Tilt your head back and feel the sun on your face. Dance under its rays. Soak in the warm energy and feel the balance restored within. Feel abundance being drawn to you. Say out loud, 'Good fortune is all around me and I invite it into my life.'

Signs: Vitality, happiness, good fortune, alignment, abundance

FOREST

Simplicity brings balance

You are being called home, to connect back to the forests and animals, where you truly belong, where everything is connected and where the life force comes from. You have a deep sense of belonging when connected to nature. The forests call to you. Don't be scared. It calls for you to rethink. It calls for you to connect on a higher level. It calls for you to just be.

Could your life be simpler? Could you strip back all the complexities that so often create drama and difficulties? What do you really need? Who do you really want to share your life with? What is nurturing you? What keeps giving and giving? What adds to your energies and fills you up with love and light? Seek simplicity and remove all else.

Balance is needed. Just as in the forest, for everything to be in harmony, there needs to be a natural order, a natural balance. Without balance there is loss, destruction and chaos. The forest is there to remind you that we all need balance and order. In which areas of your life could you find more balance? Seek the trees if you need to reconnect with what is really important to you.

Exercise:
Get into the forest and do some tree-bathing. Soak up the energy that is held there. Find a tree that is calling to you and sit next to it. There, think about what you really need and what you really want. How could you create a simpler life while still having your needs and wants met? Think about your life as a whole. Do you need to find more balance? How could you start achieving it?

Signs: Balance, simplicity, connection, realignment

AIR

A time to focus

The air element is about using your logic and intellect. It calls you to settle, breathe in life and find calm. This will help you to get into your logical mind, so you can make an important decision. Don't let your emotions control you right now. Instead, look for clarity through your breath.

If you have an unsettling feeling, it is time to question the narrative around you. Let your intuition guide you to find the answers you need. Though it can be hard, try not to get swept up in emotions. There might be more than meets the eye right now. Be flexible and open to change.

Air connects you to the deep wisdom you hold within. Using your breath, you can connect with that wisdom to help you make decisions.

The decisions you make will be about new beginnings and could help you remove blockages on your life's journey. Listen closely to the universe, to God and choose to follow the pure light that is brought to you by your wise mind. Be open to receiving messages from the divine, from spirit guides or from those passed over to help you with your decision making.

Use the lightness of air to help you organise, pulling from the energy of clarity and logic. Get everything in order to avoid chaos. Be disciplined with your time. Set up some schedules or structure to your day so that you include time to meditate to bring in that focus you need.

Exercise:
Chanting is a wonderful way to channel the air energy, allowing you to focus. Take a deep breath in through your nose, breathing in life. Feel blessed to be alive. Exhale slowly and chant, 'Om' for as long as you can as you breathe out. Feel the energy vibrate in your throat. Feel the connection to your soul, to the divine and everything around you. Breathe in peace and clarity. Repeat as many times as feels good for you.

Signs: *Clarity, focus, logic, intellect, decisions, wisdom, change, discipline, structure*

FALLING APART

Allow it all to fall away and rise above it

Everywhere you look is chaos, drama and craziness. Everything seems hard. Relationships can feel rocky and painful. Everything you thought was set in stone is now up in the air. Everything is crumbling around you. You can't make decisions. You don't know where to turn or what step to take.

This falling apart is essential. As parts of your life crumble and disintegrate, new spaces open up. Often this falling apart is needed for your elevation in a spiritual sense. Your vibration is now set higher, and you no longer gel with the things with which you were once surrounded. Even though it feels awkward, this is a good thing. You are on the move, lifting higher.

Don't try to piece it all back together. Allow the crumbling and let go. Understand that the universe is working for you. If you resist, nothing will change and the unease around you will continue.

Why does this keep happening to me? Understand this is a process of transformation. Once everything falls apart, you can start again with a new space. This can be filled with new love and light, and relationships that resonate with your higher state of consciousness. It can be filled with bigger hopes and dreams, and with abundance.

Exercise:
Take some time to meditate on acceptance and peace. Stop fighting. Stop resisting. Open up your heart and accept what is in this moment. Acknowledge that this time will pass, that new times will come with peace and fulfilment. Be open to that. Draw in hope of the future and push aside the fear of change.

Signs: Change, transformation, decisions, higher vibration

MOTHER EARTH

Give thanks and be open to her lessons

Mother Earth gives and gives, always providing, asking nothing in return and never giving up. She has a strong will, which completes what needs to be accomplished, no matter the odds. You can see it everywhere. Just look at that tiny plant sprouting in between the cracks in concrete, growing no matter the obstacles.

She understands the balance we share and how we depend on each other. Her network of energy reaches from one thing to another, from soil to plant, plant to bird, and so on. We are all connected and one. Understanding the balance means understanding our own networks, which support us, guide us and nurture us.

She provides constant lessons. What lessons are being laid out before you now? What is Mother Earth trying to teach you? Look to her to help you grow. She is resilient and a direct connection with the divine. She doesn't battle with who she is, she trusts and knows what she needs to do. She doesn't shy away from hard work to achieve her true potential.

Is there work you need to do? Draw strength from Mother Earth and use it to push yourself to do what is needed. Feel grounded and supported by her. She is always there with you, ready to share a new lesson.

A strong sign of fertility, Mother Earth is always bringing in new life, but never rushing. Everything happens at the right time. You cannot rush nature and you shouldn't rush yourself. We grow just as we should and at the right time. Be patient and remember everything is happening for you.

Exercise:
Mother Earth provides so much for us. We can marvel at all the ways in which we receive from her. Sharing gratitude for all she provides will welcome in new prosperity. She knows only of abundance. Thank her deeply. Celebrate the changing of each season as a way of celebrating Mother Earth. You can do this in any way that feels right to you. It might be a feast with those you love, or it may be through prayer or an offering.

Signs: Fertility, abundance, prosperity, connection, determination, season, rituals

LEAP OF FAITH

You don't need all the answers, instead have faith

Step out into the unknown with the belief that God or the universe is working for you. Sometimes there isn't a clear path ahead but understand this is a test of your faith. There is a specific journey for each of us, but sometimes we can only see a few steps ahead. Understand that you do not need to see the entire path. Just keep walking.

Often our need to stay safe and not fail keeps us from realising our dreams. We stop ourselves from taking another step until we can see further ahead. Our journey is then stalled. We become stuck in a rut, repeating patterns over and over, and not progressing. If only we could just trust and move forward.

What if you try and fail? What is failure but a valuable lesson? Could that be the lesson you need in order to progress on your path? Never be afraid to fail. Some failure is guaranteed along the way towards fulfilling your dreams. Don't give up – instead take that failure, learn from it and keep going.

What if you risk it all and succeed? It's never too late to give something new a try. What have you longed to pursue? What do you have a passion for? Can you turn that into something that can enable you to spend your days doing what you love?

Maybe, the leap you need to take is to tell someone something. Speak your truth.

Time to hand over the worry and fears that are holding you back. Let go of the control. Nothing is certain. Life is short so don't let the potential opportunities pass you by.

Time to just go for it! Time to leap!

Exercise:
What actionable steps could you take to enable you to progress on your journey? Write down the steps. Set your intentions then use all of your effort to move forward. Acknowledge the courage it takes then trust the universe to catch you. Say out loud, 'I choose courage over comfort. I believe fully that the universe will support me.'

Signs: *Fate, chance, opportunities, lessons, risk, believe*

PAUSE

Take some time and wait

We want everything now but waiting can reveal more to us than we could ever know. Maybe we aren't ready to receive the answers. Maybe right now is a time to hold, to take a breath and be patient. The answers will come when the time is right.

Pushing ahead could be futile. Think about times when you've tried to get something done when you've been in the zone. Now think about when you've tried to do the same thing when you haven't been feeling it – it takes twice as long as when you're in the zone, right?

Sometimes it is better to wait for the right energy to present itself. Don't waste your energy by trying to push through. Instead, be still, take a moment and gather your thoughts. Find some stillness within you. Find some peace in the space between now and where you want to be next.

Wanting to know the answers, wanting to know what to do, which direction to take, can be all consuming. All that wanting can prevent you from accessing the answers that are there if you just stop. Let the answers reveal themselves to you as they should and at the right time. Stop forcing the energy to come. Make space for new energy by clearing all the thoughts of wants and desires.

Often, when you don't make a decision, the right course of action reveals itself anyway. In the pause, the answer becomes clear. Just wait.

Exercise:
If you have ever learned Transcendental Meditation, now would be a suitable time to use it, as it is a form of meditation that allows an emptiness of thoughts, a stillness of the mind. If you haven't learned it, try finding a form of meditation that focuses on the breath or clearing the mind to find stillness, quiet and space.

Signs: *Patience, lessons, stillness, peace, wait, hold*

DESIRE

What do you truly desire?

Ask yourself what is it that you want right now. Look deep into your heart and soul. Are you holding onto past desires or even what other people want for you? It can take time to realise what you really want. Once you find it, allow that passion to fuel you forward. Use desire as a motivational force to attain what your soul wants.

Be careful of all your desires. Your soul desire will want something that will leave you feeling content, but it will not lead you towards an insatiable goal or want that leaves pain in its wake. Seek out pure soul desire that, once attained, leaves you in a place of meaning and contentment. Even better, acknowledge that you may never achieve true fulfilment but commit to enjoying the process of working towards that which you desire.

Are you ready to bring forth your soul desire? It is time to manifest and put all your energy into it in order to satisfy something deep within. Often, this will come by way of serving or healing others. Perhaps you need to push yourself out of your comfort zone in order to try something new.

It's time to make a commitment with yourself to finally stop putting off doing the things that light your soul on fire. It's time to start putting some time aside to invest in yourself.

Exercise:
Take a moment to write down what you want from yourself as a person, how you wish your life to be, where you want to live, what you want to be doing with your time and who you wish to spend time with. This may be harder than you think. Return to your notes the next day. Can you refine them? How does it feel to you now some time has passed? Keep working on them, refining them and use them to remind you to focus on what you want from your life.

Signs: Focus, motivation, passion, goals, fulfilment, work

RETREAT

Step back, get some space, set boundaries

It's time to retreat into your safe space. Boundaries are needed now to protect you from others, who could be using or mistreating you. This is a time to catch your breath and refocus, to withdraw your time and energy.

Sometimes we can be unaware just how much other people around us can affect our energy. Take time to notice how you feel after spending time with certain people. Do you feel energised or drained? Once you understand how people make you feel, choose to spend more time with those who make you feel energised. If you are overly sensitive and/or an empath, this is an exercise you should use regularly, as you are more likely to soak in energy that doesn't belong to you.

Remember that you do not always have to be available for others. Healthy boundaries mean space for you too. It means being able to say, 'no' and for that to be an acceptable answer. You don't have to provide excuses. You shouldn't always say, 'yes' just to keep the peace.

Retreat, take time to think about what works for you and what doesn't. Invite others to love you even when you set boundaries. You will soon see who has expectations of you and who loves you unconditionally.

Exercise:
Imagine a boundary of light energy around you like a shield, and in one hand imagine you have a sword. Swing the sword around and above you in order to cut the cords of energy others have attached to you. Send that energy back with love. Release yourself from others so you can rest.

Signs: Boundaries, saying no, energy refill, rest, recharge

SPIRIT GUIDES

They are with you now and always

We all have spirit guides, and they manifest in many different forms – angels, animals, mythical creatures, wisps, voices, light energy, passed loved ones, or even great teachers.

Your spirit guides are with you. They are helping to guide you to achieve what you came here for. Gentle nudges can turn into hard knocks as they try to alert you on your true path. They are also there to support you and comfort you as you grow spiritually. Along your path, they can teach you and reveal messages to you if you are open to receiving them.

At times, we can all feel isolated and alone – not just physically, but mentally too. Our spirit guides are there to assure you that you are never alone. You are loved and supported. Sit still for a moment with your eyes closed. Feel the love that dwells deep within you. Let it start filling every part of your body. This love is always there for you.

A feeling of emptiness could be a sign to reach out to your spirit guide for much needed guidance when you are lost. They are there to return you back to your path, and to give you meaning and purpose again. Seek them out.

Exercise:
Before you go to bed, say a little prayer and ask for your spirit guide to reveal themselves to you. Give them thanks for the love, support and guidance they offer. When you wake, write down in a notebook anything you remember from your dreams. Keep doing this for a few weeks and see if anything starts to appear and reveal itself to you.

Signs: Teacher, revelation, lost, purpose, guidance

BOUND

Time to free yourself

Toxic bonds: Are you being controlled by your own emotions of fear, overwhelm or worry? Are you feeling restricted, trapped or unable to do what you wish? This could be a feeling of being trapped in a situation or relationship. An intense feeling of wanting to flee, but being unable to, can be overwhelming.

Addictions and habits could be separating you from your soul purpose and preventing you from connecting with your intuition and being absolutely free. Disconnection drives us to fill a void, often with things that disconnect us even more. However, that connection can be revitalised through transforming ourselves. This will help us achieve ultimate freedom.

With ultimate freedom, we are no longer slaves to our thoughts and behaviours. We can transcend and allow our soul to be elevated beyond the chains that bind us – the bonds of addictions, unhealthy habits and toxic relationships.

Unshackle yourself from the bonds of toxicity.
Unshackle yourself from that which is limiting you and preventing you from reaching your true potential.
Unshackle yourself from that which is keeping your soul from soaring.
Unshackle yourself from your own toxic thoughts.

Spiritual bonds: You might be spiritually bound to another. This bond might be greater than the life you are experiencing in this moment. Perhaps you are bound to another who is no longer in this life. They could be reaching out to you, sending you love in this moment.

You might be experiencing a spiritual bond with someone in this life. This closeness lifts you up and connects you at a much deeper level. Keep these people close as they might be spirit guides, people who have walked with you before, helping you on your journey.

Exercise:
Sit with this question: Do you feel bound at all? Does this bond feel spiritual or toxic? Ask your intuition for guidance. If the bond is toxic, imagine cutting away any cords that connect you to the person or experience. With each cut, feel a sense of increased freedom, then send the cords back to the person or place with unconditional love. If the bond is spiritual, give thanks for the love and support you are receiving.

Signs: Relationships, spirit guides, boundaries, restricted, unshackle

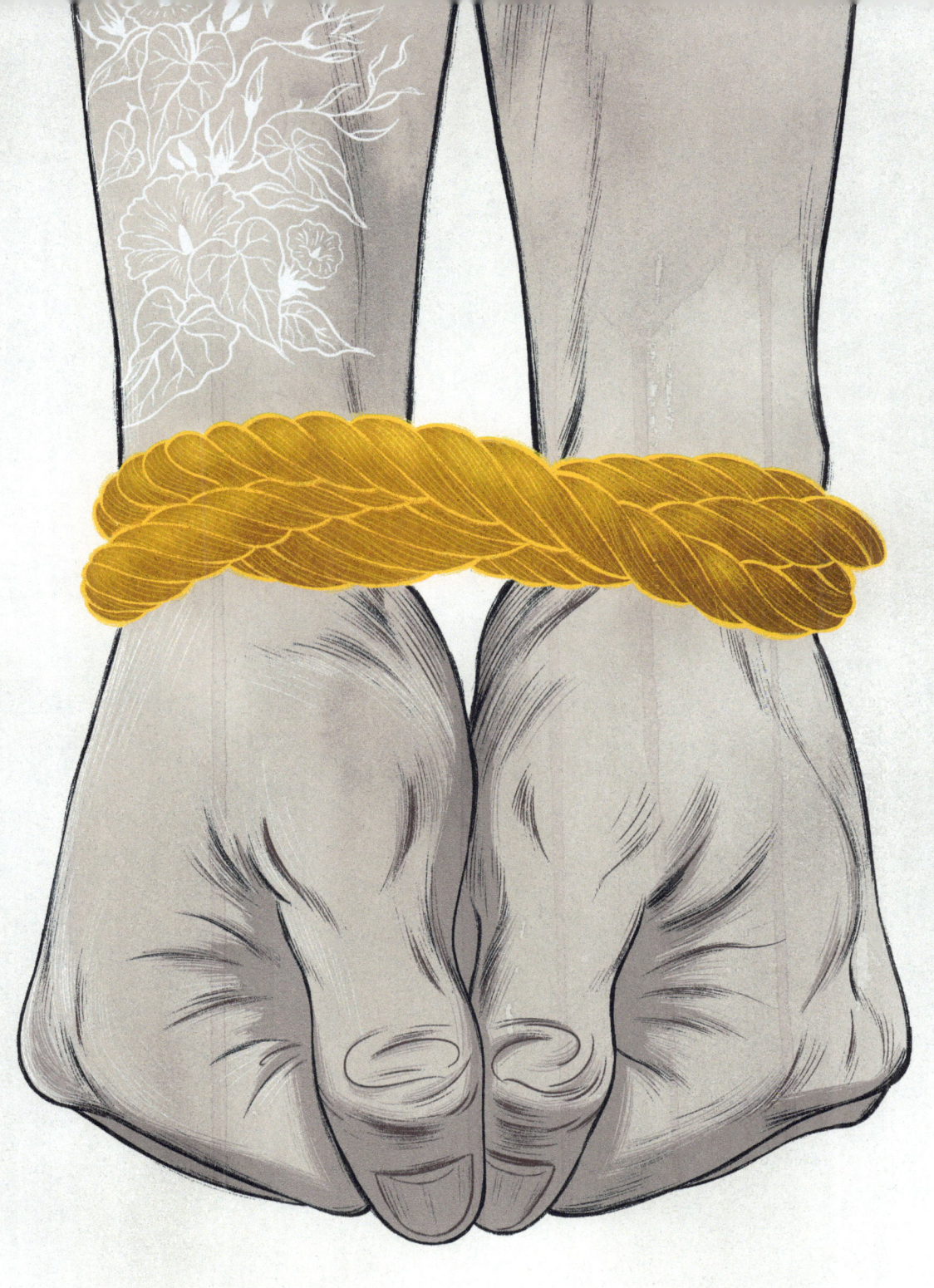

A POTENT TIME

Time to manifest

You are limitless energy with abundant potential. Once you start accessing your true power, you will begin to see what you are capable of. You are constantly creating using your energy, thoughts, emotions and actions. You are doing this all the time, even if you are not aware of it. Most people are unaware. This is a time to be conscious of what you are manifesting. What are you focusing your energy on?

This is a potent time, and it becomes more potent when you begin to witness your creations. This can happen when you start seeing synchronicities or signs that really astound you. 'Did I do that?' might pop into your head, or you might start noticing coincidences. It is like the universe is showing you these things to confirm that you indeed are creating. The more you notice, the more you start to believe in your own power. You can create more than you could ever imagine.

It is all about your intentions. Try being intentional as you move through each day. Ask yourself: 'Is this bringing me closer to the future that I desire?'

Forget about where you are now. Do not let the present limit you. Start dreaming of the future. Start living for the future and let go of the past. Rise above your desires for materialistic things and connect with your potent spirit within.

Exercise:
Set aside some time each day to focus on what you want your future to be like. Imagine your future with all the people you want to be there. Add in as many details as possible. Really feel all the emotions as you imagine your future life.

Signs: Intention, manifesting, creation, creativity, protection

SYNCHRONICITY

See the signs around you

The universe is sending you signs. They are all around you. Notice them. Things are repeating and aligning, letting you know that you are on the correct path. Your God is reaching out to let you know that you are seen and loved. Do not doubt the messages that are being sent.

You may see repeating numbers. You may see repeating patterns. You may hear a random song that calls to your soul, so take notice of its lyrics. You might even see an actual sign, quote or phrase that speaks to you. These signs let you know that you are connecting with your intuition.

Your energy is aligned with your thoughts, and you are enormously powerful when this happens. Look to your future, filled with abundance and love. It is time to create and tune in. You are in the right place, and everything is unfolding as it should. Allow your emotions to connect with what your future looks like, really pull in the energy of love and of joy.

Use your thoughts wisely. Accepting that everything is happening for you and not to you. Your path is exactly as it is meant to be so that you can grow and become more connected with who you really are. Your soul is here for a reason, and these signs are letting you know you are on track. You are supported, seen and so loved.

Your path may be in a shifting stage or a stage of growth. This is for the greater good. Your prayers and questions are being answered all around you. The more you notice these answers, the more they will reveal themselves. This is a true connection with yourself and the divine.

Exercise:
Ask your God or the universe to send you a sign then look out for it. This time don't set any intention around what the sign could be but understand and trust that you will know it when it happens. Be aware that it could be sent in the most unexpected of ways.

Signs: Manifestation, abundance, blessings, answers

REBIRTH

Shed the layers of the old you and be reborn

As you travel along your path in life, you may notice that your views, the things that are important to you and your relationships change along the way.

You may have become uncomfortable within yourself as what you project to the outside world has begun to feel empty and meaningless. You might ask yourself, 'Who am I? What am I here for?'

This is a time to rebuild, leaving the old behind and creating something new. It s an awkward time that requires a lot of tenderness. Take time to grieve the loss of the old you as you slowly let go but be excited about the updated version of you that is unfolding.

Understand that even your body is being reborn, that there are changes happening on a cellular level as you elevate to a higher level of frequency. Old patterns and trauma are no longer controlling your life. As you grow and heal from your past experiences, so too does your physical body.

Rid yourself of leftover emotions from past experiences that may muddy the water ahead. Step out as the fresh new you and show yourself to the world. Some may not like it. Relationships with those who cling onto the outdated version of you may fade away. As the new you rises, new friendships and relationships may blossom.

You can change your path and direction while growing into an updated version of yourself. Be reborn!

Exercise:
Th s is an exciting time to cleanse not only your body and mind but your surroundings too. Clear out your home and spiritual spaces. Hold an object and it will let you know if you need to keep it or not. Let go of anything that doesn't energetically pull you to hold onto it. As you clear out and cleanse, you allow room for the new. Who is it you wish to be? What is it that is important to you now?

Signs: New path, change, evolution, rebuilding

SILENCE

No words are needed

Inner silence: The world has become so noisy. There are so many distractions that constantly busy our mind and keep our ego on the main stage. Society encourages us to be busy, with an exploding diary of meetings, events and social engagements thought to signify a full life. We are bombarded with so much news, much of it scary, while social media brings with it the pressure to be perfect.

The chaos we live in has become 'normal', but we need to turn off the noise of the world and of our mind. All that noise means we cannot see or hear our inner wisdom clearly.

When we are silent, in body and mind,
we hear more, we notice more,
we feel the energy around us and within us more intensely,
we can slow everything down,
we can truly be in the present moment

Outer silence: There's no need to speak or argue your point, no need to add to your mind clutter with your own noise. Words can be used as weapons that can cause harm and conflict, which affects the energy around us. Retreating into your own physical silence means not disturbing the energy, thereby lessening the conflict in your life. So many things can be conveyed without speaking – a lasting hug, a genuine smile, a loving gaze.

Silence is powerful, it is healing and in silence you can find answers you might never have heard through the noise of the world.

Exercise:
Step into the silence and stay for a while. No words or sounds from you, no mind noise either. See if you can set aside a time each day to be silent while taking a nature walk, sitting in your garden or curled up in a comfy chair.

Signs: *Silence, stillness, healing, go slow, conflict*

BREAKTHROUGH

New opportunities are coming

It's time to elevate to a higher level. It's time to be open to the new opportunities coming your way. We are all divine creators, and when we connect with the depth of our soul essence, we can be whatever we want and need to be. With meaning and passion, we can transform into the person we want to be in order to drive us forward.

During your life, you've been handed labels about yourself. Perhaps you're 'not academic', 'not creative', 'not imaginative', 'shy', or any one of hundreds of other things we get told about ourselves. What labels have been attached to you throughout your life that could be holding you back?

Don't allow yourself to shut off from things that you could do or who you could become because of the labels that you have accepted from others. These limiting beliefs are doing just that – limiting you.

Shake those labels and limiting beliefs away. The more you let go of the labels, the more you will trust yourself and allow yourself to evolve and be open to the new opportunities that the universe presents to you. You can do things that you never thought possible.

If we close ourselves off because of limiting beliefs, we can also close ourselves off from seeing new paths, new opportunities or even that breakthrough that comes to us via dreams, ideas, or meeting new people who could help us create something new. A new business, an organisation, a movement ... who knows what breakthrough is right around the corner for you. Be open to it!

Exercise:
Sit quietly and meditate to still your mind noise. Say to yourself, 'I am open and ready to receive messages from the universe or God. I know that a breakthrough is close, and I will look for signs to help me see new opportunities.' At night, before you go to sleep, write in a note book for a few minutes. Jot down anything that pops into your head. A breakthrough may appear as you get ideas out of your head and onto paper.

Signs: Transformation, evolving, new stage, new perspective, breakthrough, new venture

SHADOW SELF

A time for discovery

Your true power comes from the entire you, including your shadow self. It is time to see yourself fully, both the light and the dark, and to acknowledge who you really are, all of you, even the parts that you keep hidden. This is an inward journey that you must take all on your own.

Your shadow self can be uncomfortable to confront. You need to accept your flaws and face your fears. Do not let others tell you how you are — this is something you need to experience and see for yourself. Holding onto the power that your shadow self can provide by way of vulnerability, strength, confidence and balance once you step into it. Acknowledge that this is also part of you. Acknowledge that this is who you are. Own it! Release the shame of your shadow self. Instead, love and nurture it.

Often our dark side has been kept so well hidden, we find it hard to see it ourselves. We accept the positive aspects of our personality and hide away what we deem to be 'unacceptable' or 'negative'. We all have a shadow self, as we all have secrets or parts of ourselves that we don't want to share.

Embrace the darker side of you — the faults, the flaws, the edginess, the craziness, the dark thoughts. All of these aspects are as much a part of what make you truly amazing and unique. Stop denying the wholeness of yourself in order to please others.

If we reject our shadow side, it will burst from us through frustration, anger, dissatisfaction and anxiety. It is time to allow it to come out into the light.

This might be time to seek help to resolve childhood trauma or past-life experiences that haven't been released.

Facing our shadow self is arduous work and, as you step in, your world can seem to unravel. You might find yourself asking, 'Why did I go there? What have I done?' but know this work must be completed in order to embrace yourself fully. There will be light again. You can accept and hold both sides close. You will be whole.

Exercise:
Think about three aspects or qualities that you love about yourself. Then think about three aspects or qualities that you keep hidden. With love and compassion, forgive yourself for being ashamed or guarded about these qualities. Acknowledge that they are as much as part of you as your so-called 'good' qualities. Say out loud, 'I am worthy of being loved. I accept myself fully. I embrace my shadow self and feel myself becoming whole.'

Signs: Wholeness, acceptance, trauma, healing, ego

CONNECTED

Everything is connected

Feel your connection with others, the world, the universe and the energy that flows through everything. Having a spiritual connection with the world around you means that often you do not need to use words.

As you tune into this connection, you may notice that you feel much more deeply, and you have greater empathy for yourself and others. There is a deep soul connection that enables you to feel the energy of others, their needs and their fears, which allows you to respond in a loving way.

Your emotions may feel more intense, and you may feel other people's emotions like you haven't before. This is a sign that your energy is lifting and you are feeling the connection with everything at a much deeper level. You will also find joy and contentment more readily than before because you are more present in your own life. Enjoy the simple things and you will become aware that the little things can be the most meaningful.

This deepening connection you are forging means you are becoming more aware that what you are putting out into the world matters. Raising your vibration will not only help you feel better but it will also positively impact the world around you.

Be intentional about the thoughts you put out into the world. As your connection to the energy around you grows and your vibration elevates, you may find it easier to accept others and respect their differences. This will help raise the energy to a more loving and compassionate level. It is through the higher vibrations of love and compassion that we will all connect as people.

There may be new relationships on the way. Someone may come into your life who you feel like you have known before, that there is a deep soul connection. They are coming to you at the right time, welcome them in. Be open to new relationships, whether that be a friendship or a partnership.

Exercise:
There is so much to be grateful for each day, so take some time to reflect on the things and people you are grateful for. You could try creating an altar or dedicating a shelf to expressing that gratitude in a visual way. On this, you could place photos of those you are grateful for. Try filling a jar with notes about things you cherish. Express gratitude as much as possible as this is a great way to show your connection and raise your vibration.

Signs: Contentment, emotional, vibration elevating, deeper connections, new relationships, gratitude

DEATH

The sacred end of a journey and the beginning of something new

Death is an ending but it isn't the end. So many fear it, but it is a sacred transition that we will all face. But, as we see all around us, death in one form brings life to another. Energy is transferred, not lost.

This transition can be witnessed often during life, not just at the very end. For example, with the death of our childhood as we move into adulthood, or the death of a relationship. Struggle and conflict can happen, and grief can arise, often without any acknowledgement of what it is we are losing as we step into a new journey. Emotions escalate and we ride waves of it as we come to an ending. We need to acknowledge the part we had in the journey and, at the same time, realise the end is here. Endings are needed for something new to begin.

Are you holding onto something because you don't want to face the end? Could you be preventing yourself from experiencing something new and rewarding, if only you could accept and welcome in the death of that stage in your life?

The lessons we learn as we transition through a phase of death, of an ending, cannot be learned any other way. They can transform our thinking and the way we live our life. The resulting growth can be remarkable.

Give yourself time to grieve, but don't stay there too long. Is there something you need to acknowledge that you have lost, which you haven't allowed yourself space to grieve for? What do you need to let go of? Maybe you are holding onto something that is a dead weight and no longer serving you. When you let go, the space created will allow you to welcome in the new.

We will experience many endings in our lifetime. Each come with a lesson but also a fresh start, a new path, a new phase. Welcome in the beginning as you farewell another chapter.

Exercise:
Journal about things you could be holding onto that are past their expiry – perhaps relationships, your career, or your environment. Could a change be on the way? It's time to think about the future, so write it all down.

Signs: Ending, transitioning, change, final phase, new beginnings

WOUNDED

Give yourself time to heal. Be gentle, be kind

Emotionally, physically, or spiritually, you are in need of healing. It's a time to seek wellness. Allow your pain space and give yourself time to heal. Acknowledging that you are in pain, that you have been carrying wounds for a long time, is the first step.

If we do not stop to heal our wounds, they will continue to damage us. The same things will keep happening and we will continue to be hurt. To stop our past wounds and memories from keeping us in pain, we need to investigate deeply what we carry within.

There are many ways we can be wounded. We can injure ourselves with our thoughts. We can allow ourselves to be hurt by others by not creating boundaries, by having expectations of others that we do not share with them, by not loving and respecting ourselves.

You have held these wounds for so long, but they are no longer needed. It's time to set them free, to stop hurting yourself and allowing others to hurt you. It is time to protect and balance yourself. Healing takes time. Move gently forward. You are loved, more than you realise. You hold strength and resilience within you.

Don't rush the healing journey, as it is a powerful process. If you discover you need to distance yourself from others who have hurt you or continue to hurt you, that is okay. You can love people from a distance and keep yourself safe. Offering love from a distance allows you to feel peace and allows for emotions like resentment and pain to be released. It doesn't excuse any behaviour but understands that love is healing for everyone.

Be open to accepting help from others. Be open to being loved by others. Seek out those who can help you on your healing journey. When you are tuned into your inner wisdom, these people may just appear.

Exercise:
Unburden yourself by speaking your hurts. Say out loud, 'It really hurt me when ... but I set that pain free as I no longer wish to carry it. I release the energy of pain connected with the past.' Shake your body gently. Shake each arm and leg. Do what feels right, moving your body to release the old pain energy.

Signs: Healing, help, boundaries, balance, protection, go slow

AWAKENING

Finally, you are waking up

It's like you have been wearing a blindfold, which has been removed and suddenly you can see. You see things for what they really are and for what is really important. You aren't interested in the pursuits of making money or being famous or powerful. Instead, you are interested in finding peace and contentment. You wish to focus instead on good values by which to live your life by – a simple life, a meaningful life.

This can be an extremely lonely transition. As you look around, others may be on a completely different journey to you. Your path may seem so far off course to everyone around you. Why you? Why now? Your soul needed you to wake up as you have been so disconnected from your source. There are soul lessons that will not be learned living like you were. You have a thirst for more meaning and knowledge, more connection but on a deeper level, none of this superficial stuff. You may wish to search for a connection with the divine, God or something that feels missing in your life.

Now that you can see, you notice how dysfunctional life is for so many. Everywhere you look, you see through the charade. You cannot unsee. You begin to question everything.

This awakening, if embraced, can transform your life, inviting in freedom for your soul. It will enable you to follow your soul's true path. You will attract new people who have also been awakened. However, it can make some existing relationships difficult as you grow and they remain on a different journey. The process can be painful and raw, but the end result will be something quite remarkable.

Exercise:
Do a spiritual energy cleanse with a smudge stick. A smudge stick can be made with herbs, like sage, and flowers from the garden. When gently burned they can clear toxic and old energy and bring in balance and positivity.

Signs: Fulfilment, meaning, growth, spiritual connection, faith

STAND ALONE

Be brave enough to do the work

Sometimes we wish that others could carry our burdens for us. We might want others to make us happy, or to change something about themselves in order for things to be better for us. The reality is we are the only ones that can change our life.

We must do the deep and arduous work. No one else is to blame for where we are or how we feel, and no one else can do the work for us. We are responsible for how we feel and how we react to others. Take ownership right now. Cast aside the blame and judgement of others. Fully step into what you can do to better yourself. We cannot hand over our wishes or desires to others. We cannot expect others to change so that our lives will change. It must come from us.

Don't wait for someone else to finally 'see' and 'change'. Make changes for yourself. This is the only way forward. Don't keep doing the same thing and hoping for a different outcome.

The work can be hard, exhausting even, but one day, you will look back and be so thankful that you put yourself first and worked on you. This is solitary work, so it's a time for pulling out everything, all the mess, then unravelling it all and putting back only what you want to keep and disposing of everything else.

Push yourself! You are stronger than you know. You can do the work, and if you do, you will be rewarded beyond your dreams.

Exercise:
Do something that pushes you outside of your comfort zone. With safe boundaries, set yourself a task that is a little bit hard. It could be starting the Wim Hof method of taking cold showers and/or ice baths. Make sure it's something that really pushes you, so you can see that you are much stronger than you think you are. Every time you push yourself, you will realise that you can do difficult things, survive and become stronger. Your power grows as you step into it — standing alone.

Signs: Strength, courage, self-development, work

WARRIOR

Strength and courage are within you

To be a warrior is to venture past the fear you hold. To be a warrior, you need to be able to push yourself into zones of discomfort to do difficult things. Pushing your boundaries allows you to understand how far you can go.

Through our struggles, we begin to understand ourselves more deeply. They help us to uncover what we can really achieve. Strength can help you rebel when you need to. It can also help create positive change.

You can handle the heat. You can do so much more than you ever thought possible as you draw on the strength and courage that lies within you. The more you push yourself, the more you will understand just how far you can go. You just need to keep pushing and striving for more. Keep taking one step after another, and trust that on the other side of fear is more than you hoped for.

To be a warrior is to be courageous, to stand up for what you believe in, to speak your truth. It means not backing down even if you are all alone. Being courageous can involve being on the front line in order to protect others, making sacrifices and dealing with the discomfort of not going along with others.

To be a warrior is to face your fears. These fears are often the signs for the path you must take. You can do this. You are strong and courageous. Don't let anything hold you back from achieving your dreams.

Exercise:
Write down some of the qualities you most admire or wish to possess. What actions can you take right now in order to start becoming the person you wish to be? What are your biggest fears? Could there be a message or sign in your fears showing you the path you need to follow?

Signs: Strength, courage, discomfort, achievements, rebel

FORGIVE

Forgive others and yourself

Forgiveness releases you from the bonds of pain energy. You do not need to carry the anger or resentment any longer. It weighs you down. It prevents you from fully experiencing life. It prevents you from really enjoying all there is ahead – and there is so much to be celebrated and enjoyed. Don't deny yourself that.

This is a time to forgive and allow yourself to move forward and spiritually grow. We can forgive in many ways, face to face, in writing, or just by forgiving within ourselves and not having to speak it. We can pass our pain over to God and ask for forgiveness in return.

When we release the pain and open our heart to forgiveness, we stop being the victim. From then on, we no longer blame others for where we are and what happens. So many hold onto bitterness, because to forgive would require taking ownership of what happens in the future.

Do you look for things that others do that might upset or offend you? Is it time to drop your expectations of others and, instead, turn your energy inwards. Focus on making changes in yourself. Being the victim and throwing blame on others is easy. It is much harder to be responsible for your own life and create change, but the harder path is the one that offers the most reward.

Do you need to forgive yourself? This could be a time to offer yourself compassion. We make mistakes and this is how we grow. Holding onto guilt or regret doesn't serve you. Find a way to start moving forward. Forgive yourself.

Exercise:
Write down on a piece of paper who you wish to forgive. Fold up the paper and place it safely on a fire and let it burn. As the paper burns feel the release of resentment and pain. Do this ritual as many times as you need to in order to find peace.

Signs: Forgiveness, compassion, healing, growth

YOUR INNER CIRCLE

Draw in close those who uplift you

It is time to come together and celebrate with your community and those you choose as your kin. They are needed now, so hold them close, fight for them, love them hard. Your inner circle helps you to grow.

There are friends who come and go and a few who stay for the long term. Either way, your inner circle is a group of people who are vibrating at the same level as you or higher. It may consist of only one or two people, but the size of your inner circle doesn't matter. What matters is how the people in it make you feel.

We all need each other, and together we boost each other up. We can lift each other's energy up in many ways – through laughter, dance, rituals or celebrations; whatever is right for your crew. It is all about bringing in joy and light. The ability to lift your energy is what your inner circle can provide. Everything feels lighter when you are together.

Make time to celebrate your circle. Regular get-togethers feed the soul. Planning feasts or rituals together reinforces your connectedness and helps you to feel supported and loved.

You can tell if someone is really part of your crew when you can be yourself fully and not feel shame or judgement. With them, you feel accepted, validated and genuinely loved on a soul level. Often, it can feel like you've known these people in another life, or perhaps your souls have met before and were close.

You deserve to be loved unconditionally. There is always someone out in the world for you. People who will connect with you where you are in this moment. Be open to welcoming new people into your world. You can choose your own family; you can decide who is your kin. It is time to bring those you want in your inner circle together and celebrate them.

Exercise:
When you are around people, consciously notice if your energy contracts or expands. Do you walk lighter or drag yourself along after spending time with them? Acknowledge if your energy has been disturbed in any way. Seek out those who leave you feeling lighter, who lift your spirits. Set a date and plan a celebration of kinship for all those that lift you up. Dance under the moonlight, go skinny dipping or light a bonfire together.

Signs: *Celebration, elevated energy, friendships, reunited, expansion, growth, family*

GATEWAY

Between two worlds, the veil is thin – someone passed is with you now

Someone passed is holding you close, loving you and shining their light on you. They want you to know they are with you in this moment and always.

They send us signs, so take notice. It could be a song playing or a scent that reminds you of them. When the sun shines on your face, know the warmth is someone you love embracing you, spreading their love over you like a warm blanket. When you notice an animal or insect that seems to be attracted to you, know it is someone you love trying to get your attention. They want you to know they are here with you. You are not alone.

When you connect deep down you will know they are with you. You are not imagining it. Never doubt yourself. Even though we are separated physically, our loved ones still exist but in another form. Remember and honour them. Acknowledge their presence and send love to them. Energy never dies, so their energy is around you always. Feel their love.

Exercise:
Light a candle for your loved one and send them a prayer. Keep a little shelf for your loved one with a photo of them and maybe something they would have loved. Speak to them. They can hear you.

Signs: Honour, connection, energy, relationships, unconditional love

GIVE & RECEIVE

Remember to be generous

Giving flows back in many wonderful ways. It is a gentle back and forth movement of beautiful energy. Success and prosperity are welcomed in when we give and receive. When we give, we wish to share what we have with others in order to uplift them.

Giving has a wonderful feeling attached to it, especially when you give without wanting anything in return. You are simply passing on a higher energy of abundance to another, and in doing so you elevate your frequency even higher. You can feel love and compassion swell inside.

You also must make space to receive, to allow others to pass this energy to you. Do not block that beautiful energy from returning by not allowing others to experience the joy of giving to you. Partake in the back-and-forth movement of love energy. Do not deny others of this giving energy, and do not deny yourself of this energy.

When help is offered, accept it. Push aside any pride and acknowledge that we all need help from time to time. Don't deny others the act of giving to you. Accept that powerful energy with grace. When you allow others to help, it is an act of love. You are allowing them to show love to you. Know that you are worthy of being helped and loved.

This is a time to give thanks and be generous. Sit for a moment and enjoy all you have in this moment. Feel the contentment. Giving and receiving radiates out energy into the field that benefits so many.

Exercise:
How can you give? Do something to help others. What can you do to help someone else? Could you cook someone a meal or babysit for them so they can go out? Maybe you could just randomly gift something to someone in the street? Maybe you could donate to a great cause? Whatever you do, be aware of doing it with love energy leaving you and transferring to another.

Signs: Giving, receiving, helping, luck, good fortune

MOON

You carry emotions that can be buried deep

The moon shines light in the darkness to help when emotions can overwhelm and cause us to become depressed or disillusioned. The moon teaches us that 'this too shall pass,' and that the darkness will not be forever, that the light of the moon will shine again. Be patient.

Tap into your intuition or psychic abilities and seek what you are holding deep within you. Things might be a little off right now. If things don't feel right, you need to take time to work through them. You could let your emotions get the better of you and steer you down a path of anxiety and fear, so try not to make any rash decisions. Understand that at times we can feel all over the place, unsettled, and that is okay. We do not need to have it all figured out, all of the time.

Trust that your instincts and your intuition can guide you to the light, that you can work through and release these heavy emotions that are drawing you down. It's time to release and heal using the energy of the moon. Go slow and easy. Take time to process all that has been locked away.

The moon can trigger your subconscious mind, so you might find that you are having vivid dreams. There could be messages hidden in these dreams. The moon represents more clarity and understanding coming your way. Use the moon's power to unlock a deeper understanding of what you need right now.

The moon also offers protection for you and your family while you do the work you need to at this time. Use this time to release unwanted fears and insecurities.

Exercise:
Get yourself out under the moonlight. If you have any crystals, take them with you, and allow the moon to charge them. Look up at the moon in awe, knowing that your ancestors have gazed upon this same moon. Feel the power and energy of your ancestors channelling through the moon and ask the moon to send you a sign in your dreams tonight.

Signs: Dreams, subconscious, clarity, understanding, insecurity, fears, emotional baggage, protection

FIRE

Change is coming. Welcome it with strength and motivation

Feel the fire within you and channel it. Use it to move you forward. Maybe you feel like you have let others put out your fire. Maybe you don't trust unleashing the fire within you again as it could be dangerous.

Use the power of fire to combat the changes ahead. Use the fire within as an energy of strength and motivation that can help you with uncertain times, with difficulties. Welcome change knowing that you are protected by the fire element.

That fire is still alight within you. It is an ember burning, waiting for you to stoke it when you are ready. Don't be afraid of the power that lies within you. Awaken it!

If the fire within you burns a bit out of control at times, learning to control and channel it into your future destiny is key. Step back and notice where your fire is being used. If it is undirected and hurting others or yourself, you need to learn to redirect it. This powerful force should be used only as a positive way forward. Use the fire to take control and channel it purposely. Make a plan, then act.

Either way, fire is powerful and transformational. Welcome the change ahead as fire's protection and passion guides you. Feel your ancestors' warmth and guidance within. The energy of fire is pushing you to act.

Exercise:
Make a tight fist then slowly open your hand. Imagine flames dancing in your palm. What do you see in them? If you can look at an actual fire, what can you see in the flames? What is it you wish to use this fire energy for? Say, 'Fire protects me, strengthens me, and helps me move me towards that which my soul desires. Allow me to move through change, as uncomfortable as it can be. I am powerful!'

Signs: Change, power, protection, passion, action, force, motivation

OBSERVER

Step back and notice

You are both an observer and a participant in your life. To be the observer, you must step back and start observing your behaviour, your thoughts and all that you do.

This is a time to really start noticing – noticing your thoughts; noticing what you are consuming; noticing how you are spending your time. What do you see? Drop any judgement and just take notes.

Becoming the observer is the first step towards making meaningful changes. Through observations, you can see patterns and behaviours that may be negatively impacting your life. You can then start making change by breaking the patterns that keep you stuck.

Being truly aware of yourself and the choices you make can transform your life. You can observe and start making changes from deep within where true change comes from. You can create new pathways in your mind, new patterns and behaviours and welcome in a whole new life.

Your thoughts are so powerful. They send out energy and attract all that you put out into the world back to you, so be careful of what you are constantly thinking. What energy are you investing in? Are your thoughts of a beautiful future filled with love and laughter? Or do you dwell on painful experiences of the past? Be the observer. Notice your thoughts then change them if you need to. You are in charge. Use your power to manifest all you desire through your thoughts.

Exercise:
Set aside time each day to observe the thoughts you are having. Are these thoughts helpful to you? Do they allow you to create and draw in positive energy or are they keeping you in a fearful or limiting mindset? Write a list of a few thoughts you would like to include in your day tomorrow.

Signs: Observe, patterns, changes, thoughts

COSMIC THREADS...

Inspiration arrives some days,
And flows upon the pages.
As soon as I think, about what I should say,
The vortex I've entered, closes...

When I think of my lack of vocabulary,
And how I'm just a nobody,
The words shrivel up and disappear
Leaving a stagnant vessel, filled with fear...

There is no room for inspiration,
when the mind is compounded with lies.
So, the threads of comic wisdom leave,
Until I open up and rise...

Time goes by, the pages are bare,
Words seem to be long, forgotten.
What was once a connection to life itself,
Seems severed and laying broken.

I'm surrounded by distractions,
And times not on my side.
I'll start tomorrow or the next day,
Or maybe I'll just hide...

I'm pulled to walk in nature,
In the sun, the rain, the snow.
The birds keep calling me outside,
So, I honour their wisdom and go...

I feel the sun upon my face,
My feet on Mama Earth.
My eyes and heart are opening,
And consciousness returns...

The strands of inspiration,
Are dancing in the sky
I hear them, see them, feel them
I'm awakening, I'm alive!

Everything seems brighter,
The sky is vibrant blue
The naked trees sway side by side
Smalls blossoms, are anew...

I sit with pen and paper,
And I welcome the connection.
My love affair with life itself
Is desperate to be spoken...

I return to where I trust in life,
And the vortex opens wide.
The cosmic threads flow easily,
This time I'm ready, for the ride...

Now I understand,
That seasons come and go.
So, while these words, flow from the heavens,
I'll be a vessel and let them grow.

My pages fill, with creative words,
Which I know aren't just for me.
So, I jot them down and humbly give thanks,
And promise to set them free...

By Tracy Manu